KIDS' WRITERS

Janet Grant

Fitzhenry & Whiteside

Kids' Writers

ⓒ Fitzhenry & Whiteside Limited 1989

Fitzhenry & Whiteside
195 Allstate Parkway
Markham, Ontario L3R 4T8

Printed and bound in Canada

CONTENTS

Canadian Cataloguing in Publication Data

Grant, Janet
  Kid's writers

(Canadian lives)
ISBN 0-88902-851-6

1. Authors, Canadian (English) —
Biography — Juvenile literature.
2. Women authors, Canadian (English) -
Biography — Juvenile literature.
I. Title. II. Series: Canadian lives
(Markham, Ont.).

PS8081.G73 1989   jc810'.9
C89-093024-4   PR9189.6.g73 1989

Editors
Bruce McDougall
Dorothy Salusbury

Designer Darrell McCalla

Picture credits
Campbell Estate 50
Ian Gillen 59
Lee Family 6-9
Little Family Cover 18-29
Macdonald Estate cover, 46-49, 53, 56, 58, 60, 61
Mead Educational cover, 3, 5, 14, 17, 37, 41, 42
Munsch Family 32-36
National Archives of Canada 52
Prince Edward Island Public Archives 51

Canadian Lives

General Editors
Fred McFadden
Robert Read

Consulting Editors
Doug Dolan
Marjorie E. White

Advisory Panel

Paul Bion	British Columbia
J.G. Bradley	Quebec
Ellen Dunn	Nova Scotia
Jean Hoeft	Alberta
Eric Norman	Newfoundland
Agnes Rolheiser	Saskatchewan
Leslie Steeves	Prince Edward Island
Mary Lou Stirling	New Brunswick
Len Zarry	Manitoba

Titles

Brian Orser	Swimmers
Jeanne Sauvé	Bravery
David Suzuki	Entrepreneurs
Laurie Graham	Kids' Writers
Bryan Adams	Painters
Karen Kain	Musicians
Robert Bateman	Track & Field
Wayne Gretzky	Pioneers

CHAPTER 1

Dennis Lee: From Alligators to Fraggles

Dennis Lee wondered if he could write some poetry for children that would include ordinary, everyday things

"What's a tuffet, Dad?" one of Dennis Lee's children asked him.

Lee scratched his head, looked down at his children through his horn-rimmed spectacles, then back at his copy of *Mother Goose*. "I don't know," he confessed.

He flipped through the pages of the nursery rhymes. Here were all the rhymes he had listened to quite happily as a child. But now that he thought of it, where were the everyday things of his children's everyday lives in Canada? Not queens and jolly millers, but hockey sticks, laundromats, sidewalks, and pizzas? They weren't to be found in the words or the pictures.

"Hmmm . . . ," Lee wondered. Could he, a poet who wrote for adults, write some new, lively, and funny nursery rhymes? Before long, Lee, who liked to sit thinking in an armchair in his study, discovered something. In his imagination there were a number of children's voices clamouring for his attention. He gave each voice an age. There were a two-year-old and a five-year-old who wanted nursery rhymes and lullabies. And there was a ten-year-old who wanted verses full of exciting and scary things.

The more Lee thought about writing nursery rhymes, the more sounds, characters' names, and fragments of poems popped into his head! Before long he had a whole collection of poems, which he published in his first children's book of poems, *Wiggle to the Laundromat*. Lee was hooked.

The kids in his imagination clamoured for more attention, and soon verses like "Give away my hockey stick, give away my hoop, but don't give away my alligator soup" danced through Lee's head. In 1974, Dennis Lee's book *Alligator Pie* was published, and it became one of the most important children's books in Canada.

Alligator Pie was a full-colour, fully illustrated children's book. It had an exciting text. It was also a very special book because it had rhymes and pictures of Canadian things:

Interview with Dennis Lee

"When I started reading nursery rhymes to my children, I quickly developed a twitch. All we seemed to read about were jolly millers, little pigs, and queens. The details of Mother Goose—the wassails and Dobbins and pipers and pence—had become exotic, but children loved them, but they were no longer home ground.

Not that this was a bad thing. But I started to wonder: shouldn't a child also discover the imagination playing on things she lived with every day? Not abolishing Mother Goose, but letting her take up residence among hockey sticks and high-rises too? I began experimenting."

Dennis's poems were filled with Canadian things and places

4

silver dollars with a Canada goose, places like Kamloops, and animals such as ookpiks.

In two years it established itself as the most popular children's book in Canada. As Bob Munsch, another famous Canadian children's author, says, "Before *Alligator Pie*, Canadian picture books were not all that exciting. *Alligator Pie* opened the door for illustrated Canadian children's books."

"Freddy the Pig" Years

Dennis Lee was born in Etobicoke, Ontario, on August 31, 1939. He was the second of four children, three boys and a girl. They were a close family. His parents were high school teachers, and taught Dennis to love words and appreciate imagination. The whole family loved to read.

As a child Dennis heard all of Mother Goose and all sorts of folk tales. He loved the rhymes. Dennis's favourite books were *Winnie-the-Pooh*, *Alice in Wonderland*, and *Freddy the Pig*. There were 15 or more *Freddy the Pig* books written by Walter P. Brooks.

Summers were special for Dennis. Dennis and his brothers and sisters would go to the library at the end of the school year in June and take out as many books as they were allowed. The whole family then left for the family's ramshackle cottage, 160 kilometres north of Toronto. Dennis liked the outdoors, the privacy to read or practise magic tricks, and the fact that his parents were there for the whole summer to play with or talk to. He considered the cottage his real home.

Dennis was shy. He liked reading or writing in a quiet place. At the age of seven he was already playing with rhymes and words. The humour of his early poetry would eventually find its way into his adult poetry. His first poem, "If", appeared in an American children's

Dennis's parents read him all kinds of children's books when he was very young

The Lee family spent summers at a cottage north of Toronto. They all read as many books as they could during the holiday. Practising magic was also a special hobby

magazine, *Wee Wisdom*, when he was seven.

If birds had horns,
If cows had wings,
If pigs had humps,
And other things . . .

The world would be a funny place
If all these things were true.
The world would be still funnier
If I were you.

Dennis played hockey, although skating primarily on his ankles made it hard for him to score. Each year, he wore through his skates at the ankles, and his parents had to buy him a new pair.

Literature Calls

Dennis attended the University of Toronto Schools, which was a boys' school with only male teachers. Dennis was a good student. Each year he contributed to the U.T.S. yearbook, called The Twig. When he was 16 he wrote a poem called "Free Verse":

And then you have big long lines that don't really mean that much
Or little
Wee short
things that
Mean even less

"Free Verse" was published the next year in 1956 in an anthology called *First Flowering: A Selection of Prose and Poetry by the Youth of Canada*.

In high school he played football and practised magic tricks. He became so good at inventing magic tricks that he thought of becoming a magician when he grew up. He settled for having some of his tricks published in magic magazines.

Dennis Lee graduated from high school with the highest marks in the province of Ontario. He was also chosen as the valedictorian in his graduating year. In his speech to the graduating class, parents, and teachers, he started, "A school is made of people — and so our memories are made up of people." He

Poetry London - New York
513 Sixth Avenue, New York 11, N. Y.

THE EDITOR thanks you for your courtesy in submitting the enclosed poems. They are returned with regrets since he is unable to make use of them.

Sincerely
Patricia Hutson
Secretary

Dennis continued to read and write as much as he could during his school years. He also submitted poetry to magazines, but received many rejection letters

VALEDICTORY, 1957

Mr. Chairman, Members of the Platform Party, Ladies and Gentlemen: One of the most certain things about anything in our world is that it is never completely black or white—it always carries some intermediate shade of grey. For example, modern scientific knowledge cannot be considered either completely good or completely harmful. And so it is when we come to leave U.T.S.—it is very difficult to analyze this peculiar mixture of nostalgia, regret and eagerness that we feel as we leave the School.

One thing we can say is that these feelings are embodied for each one of us in our memories, memories that come flooding back to us whenever we think of our school. And what we remember first is a combination of the very moving experiences we had, and the almost trite ones.

We think of the nervousness we all felt as we tried the examinations to enter the school—and which five years later, we felt in no less measure as we wrote the exams to leave it. And it was not until we had completed the final one, that we stopped to think what the School really meant to us.

D. B. LEE
VALEDICTORIAN

Dennis's sense of humour always came through, even in his valedictory speech

mentioned some of the highlights of his high school years: learning such useful things as the song "Love and Marriage" in Latin. When he was in grade 12, he said, a teacher had saved the lives of the 400 boys at U.T.S. — he had put the cafeteria under different management.

Lee chose to study at Victoria College, part of the University of Toronto. Margaret Atwood, who was also studying there, remembers dancing with Lee and working together on the college's literary magazine. She describes him then as having a worried look, but an outrageous sense of humour.

Lee had originally planned to become a minister. But during his studies of English Literature, he changed his path. In 1963, Lee decided to remain at the college teaching part-time and completing his next degree, a Master of Arts in English. He says it took him 10 years to realize he wanted to be a writer.

acta victoriana

Acta Victoriana is the Victoria College Literary magazine. Dennis contributed poetry to the magazine regularly

THE HOUSE OF ANANSI

"A FORCE TO BE RECKONED WITH
ON THE CANADIAN PUBLISHING SCENE"
—*The New York Times,* May 1969

Publisher, Editor, and Poet

The House of Anansi helped many young Canadian writers get their start

In 1967, Lee tried his hand at publishing. He started a small publishing house with a friend. It was called The House of Anansi Press. Lee selected and edited manuscripts from school friends like Margaret Atwood. He also worked with Graeme Gibson, Marian Engel, and Al Purdy, all prominent Canadian writers. During this time he also developed a reputation as an excellent editor.

At age 30, Lee published his first important work of poetry for adults, *Civil Elegies.* An elegy is a sad, meditative poem. His book was a series of poems about the problems of living as an adult today. *Civil Elegies* was published again in 1972 in a revised, expanded edition, and it won the Governor-General's Award for poetry.

Dennis's book of poems, *Civil Elegies,* won praise from readers as well as a Governor-General's award

In subsequent years Lee has worked at a publishing house, and was writer-in-residence at Trent University, the University of Toronto, and Edinburgh University, in Scotland.

Dennis Lee had never thought of writing anything for children until his daughters asked him about the tuffet in "Little Miss Muffet". He then remembered the joy of reading folk tales and Mother Goose, and wrote some poems about Canada. He put Bloor Street and Kamloops and Napanee in his poems. He thought that was rather daring at first, but everyone seemed to love it, so he did more.

Little Miss Dimble

Little Miss Dimble
Lived in a thimble,
Slept in a measuring spoon.
She met a mosquito
And called him "My sweet-o,"
And married him under the moon.

9

Lee wrote *Nicholas Knock and Other People*, *Garbage Delight*, *The Ordinary Bath*, and *Lizzy's Lion*, all illustrated by Canadian artists. In another of his books, *Jelly Belly*, he created poems that played on all the old poems of Mother Goose. For example, he answered his daughter's question about a tuffet with a poem, "Little Miss Dimble". Little Miss Dimble lived in a thimble, rather than Miss Muffet who sat on a tuffet. This little miss wasn't frightened away by a spider — she wasn't even frightened away by a mosquito. In fact, she married one.

Jelly Belly is a collection of poems based on the more traditional poetry of Mother Goose

Rocking with the Fraggles

Dennis Lee once told the Children's Book Centre in Toronto that there were two things he would love to do: draw pictures and write songs. "I can't draw my way out of a paper bag", he said. "And while I can hear music in my head (and play it on the piano), my voice is so wonky, I can't stay on key or carry a tune." He concluded sadly, "Those are two ambitions I will never realize."

Lee had always been a fan of jazz musicians, though, and in 1981, Jim Henson made Dennis draw on his untapped musical skills. Henson, creator of The Muppets, asked Lee to write some lyrics for a new TV series called *Fraggle Rock*. Phil Balsam was to compose the tunes. Dennis loved writing songs, and his wonky voice wasn't a problem, because he didn't have to sing them. Lee and Balsam wrote songs like "Catch the Tail by the Tiger", "Beetle Song", and "Wemblin' Fool". Lee wrote more than two songs a show for 56 shows!

Lee also wrote the verses for Mordecai Richler's children's book, *Jacob Two-Two Meets The Hooded Fang*. He was asked to help write the story for Jim Henson's movie, *The Dark Crystal*, a $25-million fantasy film, which appeared in 1982. Henson also asked Lee to write the screenplay for another fantasy feature

THE DARK CRYSTAL

Ticket at front desk.

Dennis Lee
97 Greensides Avenue
Toronto, Ontario
M6 G3 P8

December 3, 1982

Dear Dennis,

Both Jim Henson and Frank Oz have asked that you be invited to the New York premiere of THE DARK CRYSTAL. I am enclosing an invitation with all pertinent information. Please disregard the date for replies and the telephone number for responses. Call me at 212 794-2400, so that I can arrange to get you tickets to all the festivities.

Kind regards,

Nancy Evans

encl.

film, *Labyrinth*. But Lee didn't pretend to know the art of screenwriting, and instead offered to write a book. Someone else could turn the book into a screenplay. Eventually Terry Jones of the Monty Python group turned Lee's book into a screenplay.

Children from all over Canada write Dennis Lee to tell him how much they enjoy his poems

John

Dear Mr. Lee

We are happy you came to our school.
Our teacher read us the book JELLY BELLY.
We Loved it! We had Lots of laugh.
Our favorite poem is "Mrs. Murphy" and Mrs. Murphys
kids.

Mr. Dennis Lee,
c/o Macmillan of Canada,
70 Bond Street,
Toronto, Ontario M5D 1X3

Salmon Arm B.C.
Elementry
School
April 25, 1983

Dear Mr. Lee
I have read some of your poems.
I like most of them because they're funny.
Some of them rhyme some of them don't.
I like your pictures a lot "I wish I could draw
pictures like you.

Your Friend
Aaron
British Columbia Carlson

The Dinosaurs' Dinner

1. Allosaurus, stegosaurus,
   Brontosaurus too.
   All went off for dinner at the
   Dinosaur zoo,

2. Along came the waiter
   called Tyrannosaurus Rex,
   Gobbled up the table
   cause they wouldn't pay
   their checks.

Box Hawkey schol
383 Big Springs Dr.
Airdrie Alber
T4M CBO
Mai 8 1984

Dear Denis Lee,
Yor poems are good.
Wer do you live? Do you live
in Las Vegas? Do you live in
Ontario? Ill tell you
wer I live I live in Airdrie
My Phone Numbr is 948 7423
I like Jelly Belly
and Alligator
pie

Jeff C.
1Ms

For many years Lee lived with his wife, Donna, and three children in a well-loved and well-worn cottage in Toronto. It was a comfortable old cottage, which sported a ping-pong table in the living room. But his children's curiosity set him on a whole new creative path.

His children have now grown up, and Lee has re-married. He lives with his second wife, Susan, in what he calls "a real house", but no matter where he tried to put it, the ping-pong table just didn't fit. Meanwhile, he still gets fan mail from adults and children alike.

Lee's favourite foods are "slushy" things, like macaroni and cheese. No one has asked him to draw his way out of a paper bag, so he still spends most of his time writing. And when he is not writing? He is "itching and twitching", because he is not writing. He follows his own advice to other writers: "Write . . . write . . . write . . . And when you've finished, write some more."

He loves to read his poetry to children, and delight them with the playfulness of his ideas and words. So far, Dennis Lee has asked us to stuff "the toes and tum and head" of any robber in the garbage, to jump in the stew because "gravy and carrots are good for you", to avoid kissing Dirty Georgie, to watch for Jacques

Dirty Georgie

Georgie's face was
Never clean,
Georgie smelled like
Gasoline.

Kissing Georgie—
Mighty fine!
Just like kissing
Frankenstein!

Georgie, Georgie,
Wash your face,
Or we'll kick you out
Of the human race:

Not because you're ugly,
Not because you're cute,
Just because your dirty ears
Smell like rubber boots!

32

Dennis loves to write and he continues to entertain children with his poems

Cartier in a tall silk hat, and definitely not give away our alligator pie. One can't help wondering what he will ask of us next?

CHAPTER 2

Jean Little: Books, Bytes, and Barks

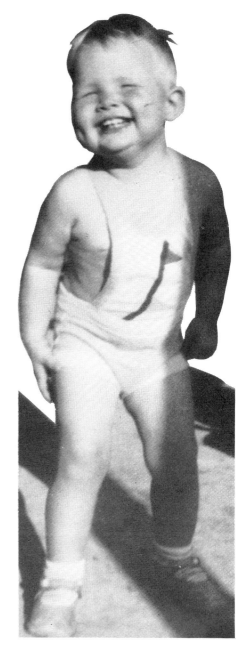

Her bad eyesight did not prevent two-year-old Jean from having fun just like other children her age

One day, when Jean Little was seven years old, she got lost on the streetcar in Toronto and rode it all the way to the end of the line. It was a journey she would never forget. But that night, while her mother read a book to Jean and her brothers and sister, Jean went on a different type of journey.

As Jean's mother read *The Secret Garden*, the story of a disagreeable-looking girl named Mary, Jean realized she wasn't alone in the world. Here at last was another girl who looked disagreeable, and was selfish and bad-tempered. But more important, here was someone who,

The Little Family in 1938. Llew and Flora Little, Jean's parents, were medical missionaries in Taiwan and later Hong Kong

despite all this, could grow into someone special. Being special was very important to Jean Little, the blue-eyed, seven-year-old girl in Toronto.

People always thought Jean was different because of her very poor eyesight. She had been born with scars on the pupils of her eyes. She turned to the light as most babies do, but did not reach for anything in front of her until she was a year old.

When Jean was born, her parents, Flora and Llew, were working as doctors in a mission in Taiwan, an island just off the southeast coast of China. Jean's mother, Flora, had also been born in Taiwan to Canadian missionaries. She had lived there for five years, then come to Canada to go to school. Later, she returned to Taiwan as a missionary, but she came back again to Canada to marry Llew Little, a doctor she had met at medical school, who had an excellent sense of humour. Finally, they both decided to become missionaries in Taiwan. Jean was born on Saturday, January 2, 1932, the second of four children. Her older brother was Jamie, and Hugh and Patricia followed Jean.

Special, Not Different

Jean's eyesight improved as her eyes grew. But she could still see only a short distance in front of her. Beyond that, the rest of the world remained blurred. Even so, Jean's parents were determined that Jean should learn to get along with children who had normal sight.

At times, Jean felt incredibly awkward. More than once she tried a trick on the monkey bars at the park, after watching other children do it, only to find she hadn't quite seen it correctly. Where other children would use their eyes to learn the trick, Jean needed verbal step-by-step instructions. But only a few children or adults realized that Jean needed this kind of help.

Just like Anna in her book *From Anna*, Jean hated being thought of as different. "Special, though, was something else", she says. "It meant wonderful, didn't it? It meant better than other people."

In the meantime, Jean developed an early love of books. One of the first words that Jean learned to say was "book-a". She loved being read to as a child. She was also very eager to learn how to read by herself.

When Jean was five, her mom set out to teach her to read and write. It was not an easy task. Jean had to walk back and forth in front of a chart of large letters that her mother had made so she could see a few words at a time. She also read books specially printed with large type, ordered from Canada.

Jean and her two brothers, Hugh and Jamie, in Hong Kong

Shortly before the Littles moved from Taiwan to Hong Kong, Jean's younger sister, Patricia, was born

When Jean was six, her family moved from Taiwan to Hong Kong. A year later, in 1938, Jean's parents moved their family to Canada to avoid the war that broke out three years later. They sailed on the *Empress of Canada* to Yokohama, Japan, then on the ocean liner *Hiye Maru* to Vancouver, Canada. Then they travelled by train across Canada to Toronto's Union Station.

Jean's first home in Canada was a house on Kingswood Road in Toronto. Her parents enrolled her in a special sight-saving class at Duke of Connaught School downtown. After a few months, the family moved to Bedford Road, and Jean went to Jesse Ketchum School. Once again, a sight-saving class made it easier for a child with poor vision to learn.

In Jean's classes, there was one huge dictionary with large print, and the teacher wrote large letters with a fat piece of chalk on a green blackboard, so all her students could read the words. Jean was allowed to sit close to the board, and she started to make friends with her classmates, who also had trouble seeing, much like Anna did with Benjamin in *From Anna*.

At Jesse Ketchum Public School, Jean was in a sight-saving class of mixed grades. She enjoyed listening to the other grades' stories and poems after she had finished her own work

Other Challenges, Other Triumphs

When Jean was eight, her family moved to Guelph, a smaller city about 70 kilometres west of Toronto. There, Jean faced one of the biggest challenges of any handicapped child — going to school in a regular school. English was her best subject; mathematics her worst. Once again, Jean had to face the prospect of making new friends. But friends luckily came in all shapes and sizes. While Jean learned to make friends among her new schoolmates, she kept the make-believe friends she had found in books.

Jean's dad, who had wanted to be a writer himself, greatly encouraged her to write. In grade six, Jean wrote her first poem. When Jean was 15, her dad privately published a volume of her poems called *It's a Wonderful World*.

Ten-year-old Jean with the family dog, Chummy. Going to a regular school was sometimes very difficult for Jean because the other children teased her about her eyes

A summer holiday at Hall's Lake — Jean is 12

Two years later, Jean wrote two poems, "Mary" and "Joseph", Christmas poems about the couple's thoughts as they approached Bethlehem. Her dad sent them off to a magazine. On December 26, much to Jean's amazement, they were published in the magazine *Saturday Night*. The poems' publication caused a sensation at Jean's school. She received a cheque for $35, which she promptly spent on material for a dress to celebrate.

Off to University

Little completed Grade 13, but says she stopped understanding math in grade nine and nearly had to repeat grade 12. She wanted to study English at Victoria College, part of the University of Toronto. She convinced the person in charge of admissions to at least let her try to pursue an English degree there. She knew it would be difficult to keep up with all the reading, but she was willing to give it her best shot.

Little wrote her first long story, "Let Me Be Gentle", during the summer following her first year of university. She submitted it to a book publisher, but it was turned down. The letter of rejection told her she had talent and

Jean lived at Annesley Hall, a women's residence, while at university. It was difficult for her to be accepted at Victoria College because of her eyesight. But she graduated first in her class

should keep writing. Little decided to keep on writing.

At university, Little recalls playing one basketball game, which was as scary as standing in the middle of a freeway in rush hour. Girls rushed around her, passing the ball and shouting, while Little could barely see. Near the end of the game, Little found a basketball within her reach and she stretched out her hands to catch it. Both teams were stunned. One of Little's teammates recovered herself and called for Little to pass the ball. Little tossed the ball in the direction of the girl's voice. The girl caught it and threw it into the hoop for the winning basket.

After completing her courses, Little graduated at the top of her class in Victoria College in English Language and Literature.

After university, Little taught at the Rotary Club's Crippled Children's Centre in Guelph. As part of her teaching, she read many books to her disabled students. That's when she noticed a large gap in children's literature. All of the disabled or ill children in the books, including Heidi, seemed to get cured almost overnight. From her own experience, Little knew that getting better overnight didn't happen for most disabled children.

VICTORIA
UNIVERSITY
The First 150 Years

AN EXHIBITION
TO CELEBRATE
Victoria's Sesquicentennial

Board Members of the Rotary Club and some of Jean's pupils present her with a gift. She was taking a leave of absence to write

Writing Full-time

Now Little wrote a book about the fears and challenges facing disabled children. She knew exactly what they were from her own childhood experiences. Top of the list was getting lost. There were other fears, as well, like meeting strangers and walking into a room alone and being stared at.

Little's book, *Mine for Keeps*, describes a girl named Sal who has cerebral palsy. Sal cannot use her leg muscles very well. But her dog, Susie, is more afraid of things than Sal, and that makes it easier for Sal to get over her fears.

Jean and her dog, Susie. Susie is the dog Jean wrote about in her first book, *Mine For Keeps*

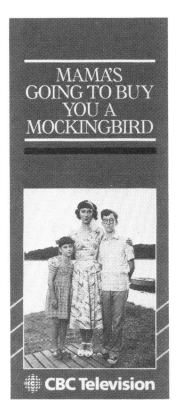

MAMA'S GOING TO BUY YOU A MOCKINGBIRD

CBC Television

When *Mine for Keeps* was accepted by a publisher, Little jumped for joy. She decided to stop teaching and write full-time.

Nine more of Little's books appeared between 1962 and 1977, starting with *Home From Far* and ending with *Listen for the Singing*. In *Listen for the Singing*, Anna helps her older brother Rudi who has been left blind by an accident. Rudi is deeply embarrassed and upset about his new blindness. But Anna, who has poor sight herself, confronts him, then helps him learn braille.

Little's next book took seven years to write. Her eyesight turned so bad, she had to dictate the book into a tape recorder. It was a very long and frustrating process, but the result was one of her most successful books. *Mama's Going to Buy You a Mockingbird* is about a boy who discovers his father has cancer. It is a moving story about surviving the death of a parent. It won two major Canadian awards, and by 1987 it had sold over 150000 copies. The CBC made a movie version of it for Christmas, 1988.

When Jean first met Zephyr, her guide dog, it was hard to learn to trust him. But she loved the dog right away and he is her constant companion

Bytes and Barks

All of the dogs in Little's novels are based on real animals she has known. In real life, Zephyr, a yellow Labrador guide dog, is her constant companion. A guide dog is specially trained to lead a blind person safely around a city, across streets and along crowded sidewalks. Little says people find it easier to start a conversation with her because of Zephyr, although his tail wagging into a neighbour's cubicle in a washroom can be a bit startling.

Little takes Zephyr with her on school visits. She has an endless supply of stories to enchant her audience. She receives over 400 letters a year from her fans. Her favourite beginning of all her fan letters is, "Dear Miss Little: Are you alive or dead?"

Students enjoy listening to Jean tell her stories

Jean Little is very much alive. She now lives with her mother in a beautiful cottage in Guelph. Her favourite colour is blue, and her favourite foods are pumpkin pie and homemade bread with butter and peanut butter. Anna and Kate are Little's two favourite characters.

Today, Little's vision depends on the light. She distinguishes by contrast. She often reads a letter by holding the paper close to her right eye, with her nose almost touching the paper.

Her left eye has been removed, and in its place is a plastic ball. A removable shell-shaped piece with a painted eye fits onto the ball like a contact lens. Her plastic eye is a great conversation piece. She cannot see through it, but it looks very much like a real eye.

Meanwhile, Little continues to write with the help of her computer SAM. SAM has a vocabulary of 70 000 words and makes re-writing much easier for her. When she meets a new friend, she gives them either *From Anna*, *Mama's Going to Buy You a Mockingbird*, *Kate*, or her autobiography, *Little by Little*.

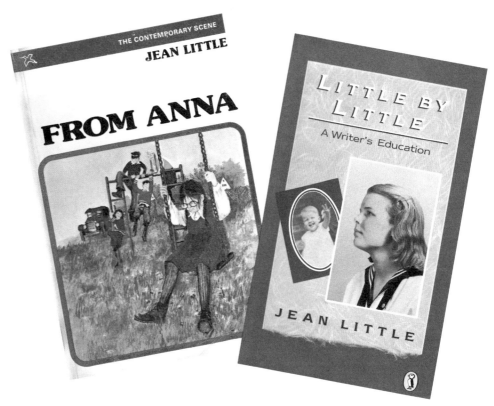

Little has now written thirteen novels, two books of poetry, and the autobiography. Most of her books have appeared in translation all over the world. She was a founding member of the Canadian Society of Children's Authors, Illustrators and Performers, a unique organization of professional artists and friends who promote Canadian children's culture.

"You can look forward to three things when you grow up," Little says. "Being in control of your own money, chosing your own bed-time, and not having to go to school." Is it worth waiting for? "You bet it is," she says.

CHAPTER 3

Robert Munsch: The UnFairy Tale Maker

Bob Munsch did not like school — not even one subject. He did not like spelling. He could not spell. He did not like doing things in groups, including sports. And he didn't like going to bed at night.

No one at school really knew what to do with Bob. He daydreamed the hours away in the classroom. He made up stories all the time. He was the hero in all his daydreams. His favourite daydream was about being Superman.

Bob did not do particularly well at school. His teachers worried that he would amount to nothing. They did not realize daydreams could turn into magical things. Only the friendly librarian, who took the time to talk to Bob, caught a glimpse of something magical

Bob in first grade. He did not like school at all

The Munsch family. Bob and his best friend, his brother, Dick, are in the centre, front row

in him. She seemed to think he might have a special talent. "Your kid is strange," the librarian said to Bob's mother, "but not stupid. He might grow up to be an artist."

Bob's father was a successful lawyer. When Bob was four, the family had moved to a new neighbourhood in Pittsburgh, Pennsylvania, where there were no children his own age. Bob's only close friend was his brother Dick. Much of the time was spent alone. One day, when he was in Grade Four, Bob looked into a mirror and said, "Kids are supposed to be happy. I am not happy." He needed something.

Saved By Books

Bob was the fourth child in a family of nine children. He was born on November 6, 1945, in Pittsburgh. In the evenings, his mother or father would read to him. His father was an avid book reader. He even made up stories occasionally. There was a library in the house, chock-a-block full of books.

Bob's father also loved to take the children out into the hills to look for fossils and identify plants. Bob even went down into a coal mine, so he had an idea of what it was like to be a coal miner.

Life improved greatly when Bob learned to read. During one summer vacation, he read over 200 books. He wore a path to the local library, borrowing books, taking them home, reading them, and returning them. His favourite book was *Bartholomew Cubbins* by Dr. Seuss.

At first Bob and the other Munsch children had to share bedrooms, sometimes sleeping four to a room, then two to a room. Finally, when Bob became the oldest boy living at home, he moved into the unheated attic on the top floor, all by himself. He was 14 at the time and loved the isolation. It gave him plenty of time to read and develop his already active imagination. Also, in a family of nine, it was nice to get some quiet time.

Bob as a baby with his mother and father

Then Bob's older brother got into trouble. "He sort of wrapped up being the bad guy of the family," Munsch recalls. (Later, he grew up to follow a successful career.) Since his older brother had taken all the excitement out of being bad, Bob decided to become the good guy of the family. He started doing well at high school, particularly because he liked history. He did so well at the subject, he went on to study it at Fordham University in New York. He then decided to study for a degree in anthropology, the study of man's origins and development, at Boston University.

Changes in Direction

While he was studying anthropology at university, Munsch decided to do some sort of community work. He started to work part-time at a daycare centre. Soon, Bob realized that he found kids more interesting than anthropology. So he quit his studies and started working full-time in a daycare centre in Boston. He also earned another degree, this time in Child Studies, from Tufts University near Boston.

Then he had a bad experience. He was living in a rough neighbourhood of Cambridge, Massachusetts, completing his studies, when one night he was attacked by a mugger who had already killed a number of people. The man attacked Munsch with a lead pipe, knocked him unconscious, and badly cut his face. The mugger believed he had killed Bob, and left him for dead. His injuries caused him to lose some of his memory. Munsch says some memories have never come back. When he recovered, he realized he was very lucky to be alive. He would now do his most to enjoy life.

Story-telling

While working in the daycare centre, Munsch told a new story to the children every day. He'd shout: "Hey, I'm going to tell you a story nobody has heard before." He says, "Usually, the

Working with children proved more interesting than studying anthropology

Bob learned some of his story techniques from watching a child in the daycare centre where he worked

stories stank. But once in a while, a really good one turned up."

One day, Munsch noticed a four-year-old boy called Jeffrey in his daycare centre. Jeffrey was a born story-teller. He was always the centre of attention. Jeffrey's problem was that he had only one story. But through watching him, Munsch picked up some useful techniques for story-telling, including slapping thighs, pulling hair, and making all sorts of good sound effects.

Over time, he improved upon these techniques, and they have become a standard part of his story-telling routine.

In the mid 1970s, Munsch and his wife accepted jobs at the Department of Family Studies at the University of Guelph in Ontario. One day, the department director heard Munsch telling stories to some children. He told Bob he should write down his stories and send them to a publisher. Soon many other people had told Munsch the same thing. Finally, he sent off fourteen stories to seven publishers. Two publishers were interested. He chose Annick Press. In 1979, *The Dark* and *The Mud Puddle* were published.

When *The Paperbag Princess* appeared the next year, Munsch had assured himself of a career as a writer. In 1982, five more of his books were published. He started working part-time at the university. Then, because he had to make so many school visits and appear in so many concerts, he became writer-in-residence at the university. Finally, Munsch decided to become a full-time story-teller and writer. This was the most important thing that fame could buy him. He had wanted to be a full-time story-teller all his life. Now he was happy.

The Dark and *The Mud Puddle*, the first books Bob published

The Making of an "Un"-Fairy Tale

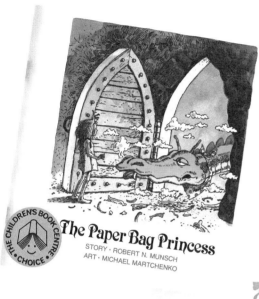

The Paper Bag Princess
STORY · ROBERT N. MUNSCH
ART · MICHAEL MARTCHENKO

Bob Munsch calls his stories "un"-fairy tales. He likes to talk about serious things in a humorous way. He takes the things he puts in a story from children's everyday lives. He then stretches the story for all it is worth. For example, five-year-old Robin in *Murmel, Murmel, Murmel* finds a baby in a sandbox and has the same conversation with five adults until she finds one who needs a baby. The princess in *The Paperbag Princess* has a dragon repeat his tricks until he drops.

MURMEL MURMEL MURMEL

Robert Munsch • M. Martchenko

Robin picked up the baby and went on down the street. She...

THE WORLD ACCORDING TO MUNSCH

It's a place of surprises, mud puddles and the dark; the kids love it

BY LIAM LACEY
The Globe and Mail
GUELPH

IN THE TOWN of Guelph lives a mild-mannered academic with a wild imagination, who makes up children's stories for a living. His name is Robert Munsch and his stories for pre-schoolers are more witty, creative and entertaining than most of what passes for adult literature.

He writes of puzzling matters, a creature called The Dark that eats shadows, a mud puddle that leaps out of trees onto unsuspecting children and a mother who drives across town at night, creeps into the room of her adult son and sings to him in his sleep. Munsch has published 15 books since he first began writing at 34 in 1978, and he is now Canada's bestselling children's author.

Anne Millyard of Annick Press recalls the day, nine years ago, when she read her first Munsch story.

"I was in the backyard looking [the] manuscripts [and] picked [...]

which won him a Juno Award in 1985.

For all his successes, though, The Fart remains unpublished. It is the story of Julie Ann, who wakes up one day to discover a big purple, green and yellow fart lying on her bed, but adults tell her this is impossible, because Canadian families don't have such things. Munsch thinks Canadian parents may feel the same way, so the story remains in temporary limbo.

Munsch revels in breaking small taboos with his books. Some of them are what he calls "family process" stories, about children's struggles for independence. Thomas' Snowsuit tells how Thomas refuses to wear his snowsuit and, when the teacher tries to wrestle him into it, she ends up wearing the snowsuit and he ends up in her dress. When the principal tries to wrestle him into it, the principal ends up in the teacher's dress and she ends up in his suit, smoking his pipe, while Thomas remains without his snowsuit.

Another "family process" story is Mortimer. A generation of Canadian parents has Munsch to blame for the popularity of this bedtime rhyme: "[...] clang, rattle bing bang [...] my noise all [...]mer, the [...]n't quite figure[...] [...]it we[...]

have Munsch stories dedicated to them.

One January morning, he has a visit scheduled for Maple Hill School, an alternative school in a log house down an unpaved country road. He dresses functionally for the visit, a toque and parka over a workshirt and baggy corduroys. As he drives, he talks, his words carefully enunciated with a deadpan delivery that always sounds as though he's leading up to a [...]

names — the name of the child about whom the story was first told. This goes against the grain in the children's book publishing business where, he says, it's considered much better marketing to write a series all around the same character.

Munsch thought he would work in [da]ycare for the rest of his life, but [lo]w pay and his disenchantment [with authori]ties led him to move to [...]

Illustrations from Mortimer (above) and Thomas' Snowsuit.

her father tries to get out the tooth with a large hammer. Still no luck. Finally t[...] [...]s get serious[...] they [...]

which work, in different ways, on both parents and children. The Paper Bag Princess is a good example. As the story ends, the princess resc[...] Prince Ronald from a drag[...] rebuked f[...] [...]

Children are the heroes in Robert Munsch books. His young characters make changes in their lives that most children cannot make. They determine with childlike logic, how to get rid of an attacking mud puddle and a shadow eater. They outsmart dragons, and find parents for babies.

Munsch's stories become books in two stages. The first stage is the telling of the story to a group of children. Sometimes, Bob tells a story for as long as three years, changing it along the way. He knows a story is good if children ask for it again and again. The children actually help him write his books. Bob deletes the parts in the story that they don't like and they help him pick the best ending.

40

First, Bob tells his stories out loud to children. Then, after many readings and re-writes, he writes the first version

The second stage usually lasts a year, when Munsch actually writes the book. First, he sits down alone and tells the story to himself. He writes a first version, without an ending. He then writes another version. He never looks back at the previous version. He does this several times. Then, much later, he re-reads all the versions. By now, the story has taken its final shape. Everything has to work: the sound of the words, the rhythm of the sentences, the pace of the chapters. Even then, his publisher will sometimes make a suggestion for the ending or the title.

Repeating Things

Munsch likes to repeat things. For example, seventeen seems to be his favourite number and the number kids find the funniest. Usually the characters in his stories do things three times. His books are fun and very well illustrated. Michael Martchenko has illustrated most of them. Munsch says he likes Martchenko's work because "it is a little crazy." The first drawings of Martchenko's that Munsch ever saw showed birds with wheels on their feet.

Michael Martchenko's drawings suit Bob — they are as funny as his stories

By 1989, Munsch had written over a dozen books, and they were enormously popular. In one year, his publisher sold close to a million copies in North America alone. Munsch has won Canadian literature awards for his books and a Juno award for his record *Murmel Murmel Munsch*. His books sell all over the world and have been translated into several languages. One recent book is called *A Promise is A Promise*, which is based on an Inuit fairy tale. Bob co-wrote it with Michael Kusugak, an Inuit story-teller. The story is more serious and traditional than many in the Robert Munsch library.

Munsch tells it like it is for kids

By Christopher Hume Toronto Star

Robert Munsch likes to tell stories. Ask any parent or child, it's something he does very well.

A soft-spoken, bearded former academic who looks like a typical Canadian slob, Munsch, 41, is the first man in this country to make his living spinning tales for children. Known internationally for his books, records and performances, he is the only star of Canadian Kid Cult who isn't a former folkie and who isn't cute.

But that doesn't seem to bother his many fans. The two concerts he's giving tomorrow at Seneca College's Minkler Auditorium were sold out within days of being announced.

"The most important thing," Munsch explains, "is to respect your audience." A father of three children who began telling stories in 1972 when he worked in a day-care centre, he not only understands his listeners but also holds them in considerable esteem.

Though he quit day-care after five years — "I burned out; too many kids, too low pay" — he never lost his passion for storytelling. He [...] ght he was doing [...] thing [...]

time writing stories than reading them.

He nevertheless accepted a job teaching in the family studies department of the University of Guelph. Then, as he tells it, "My boss called me in and said, 'What's all this record stuff and long-distance calls? What are you, a performer or a professor?'

"The light dawned. 'I'm a performer,' said Munsch. 'And I quit.'" That was three years ago but he remains an adjunct professor, which means he has "an office but no pay."

After his first book, The Dark, came out in '79, Munsch began to grow more interested in writing than performing. The 15 titles that have appeared since, most published by Toronto's Annick Press, have been sold by the hundreds of thousands throughout the English-speaking world. His most recent effort, Love You Forever, was released last October and already 30,000 have been sold. The success of Paperback Princess, one of his best-known titles, is even more astounding. Half a million copies have been bought since it was first publi [...] in 1980. Last year, 376,000 books by [...] sold in total.

[...] ke about two ye [...] get [...] "Th [...]

slowly. The plot remains but the phrasing, wording and cadence are worked on continually."

Munsch also explains that each story is written with a specific child in mind. Often they are his own but not always. Thomas' Snowsuit, for instance, was based on an incident that happened when Munsch was performing in Halifax.

It is also a tribute to his ability that his tales can be compelling for all age groups. Perhaps the best example is Love You Forever, a story in which a mother crawls into her son's room every night and whispers to him that she will love him forever. They both grow older and by the end of the book, the son is telling his aged mother — as well as his own son — that he will love them forever.

As Munsch points out, "this book has a different feel to it. It's sad for adults who see it as a story about loss but happy for children who see it as tale of role reversal."

That [...] plac [...] [...] uccess of his books, Munsch [...] d write more. Tomorrow's [...] probably he [...] in [...]

Munsch wants to be regarded as a modern-day Hans Christian Andersen. He is a superb story-teller, and amazes children and adults alike with his ability to make up stories on the spot.

Meanwhile, Bob still lives in Guelph with his wife and three children. He rents a television instead of owning one, so he can threaten to send it back. His favourite colour is black. His favourite foods are curry and Indonesian soya sauce. His favourite among his own books is *Love You Forever*. But all his tales began in his daydreams as a schoolboy, many years ago.

Bob's favourite book is *Love You Forever*

CHAPTER 4

Lucy Maud Montgomery: Never Give Up

The fourteen-year-old girl with pretty brown hair and lively brown eyes slammed the door of the wood-burning stove. Inside was the diary she had kept since she was nine. Outside, the November winds blew against the wooden frame home. Winter came early to Prince Edward Island.

She wiped her hands against her apron and returned to her bedroom. She pulled out her new diary, and looked at it with satisfaction. She was nearly fifteen. It was a time for a new beginning, she told herself.

She sat down, as she had every day since she was nine, and started to write. Not to write daily in a diary would be as bad as not washing her face or not saying her prayers. This time, she promised herself to write only about important

Lucy Maud Montgomery, age 11. Lucy first tried writing poetry when she was nine years old

things: her favourite places, her cats, school events, and books. Why? Because Lucy Maud Montgomery dreamed of becoming a great writer.

Cavendish, P.E.I.

Lucy Maud Montgomery was born on November 30, 1874, in a little village called Clifton on Prince Edward Island. She disliked her full name. She preferred to be called "Maud." When Maud was two years old, her mother died. Her father left her with her grandparents and made trips to Massachusetts and Saskatchewan in search of work.

Photograph of my father and mother taken about time of their marriage. L. M. Macdonald

Alexander and Lucy Macneill, Maud's grandparents. Maud went to live with the Macneills when her mother died

Maud lived with her grandparents, who were strict Presbyterians, in the old Macneill homestead in Cavendish, P.E.I. It was a white farmhouse with green shutters and a dark green roof, surrounded by apple orchards. Although her grandparents loved her, they did not show her a lot of affection. They also enforced very strict rules. Maud had no friends to play with until she was six.

The beautiful countryside of the island delighted Maud. She wrote, "Lands have personalities just as well as human beings." It was rich with buttercups and wild roses and other flowers. The seashore was only a kilometre away from where she lived. There she could watch the gulls and the glorious shades of sunsets.

The Macneill homestead

Maud was expressive, imaginative, and impulsive. Her warm heart created close friendships. She loved visiting her dad's relatives at Parks Corner and playing with her school friends. With her friends she played pranks, had all-night talks, and shared superstitions. Maud wrote about one in her journal: "One of our school superstitions is that if you count nine stars for nine continuous nights, the first boy you shake hands with afterwards is to be your future husband." Maud never had the patience to try it out.

School was conducted in a simply-constructed white building with tall, thin windows. Students were expected to memorize long passages of verse and prose by heart. One winter, the school was so dirty, the students decided to clean it themselves — blinds, maps, desks, windows, doors, floor, and the stove. Maud liked school in winter, but not in summer. And she liked writing compositions better than doing arithmetic.

Maud loved to read and to write. Her grandparents were not keen on Maud bringing friends home, so books became her friends. She felt that books were a world in themselves, "their characters as real as my friends of actual life", she wrote. She liked Hans Christian Andersen's fairy tales, ghost stories, and novels. She also wrote continually in her journal, which she affectionately called her "grumble book". It was a place for her to sort out problems and write down feelings she didn't feel comfortable talking about.

Maud was very bright, opinionated, and determined to publish her writing. When she was in her early teens, she sent her first poem to a magazine in the United States, but it was rejected. A year later, she sent the verses to her local paper, but the paper was not interested in them either. At an early age, Maud had learned what she called "the first, last, and middle lesson of writing — never give up!!"

Growing Up

When Maud was fifteen, she travelled nearly 5000 kilometres across Canada by train to live with her father and his new wife in Prince Albert, Saskatchewan. On her train trip, she met Sir John A. Macdonald, the Prime Minister of Canada.

Unfortunately, her father's new wife made home life very difficult for Maud. She had to keep house, take care of her new baby step-brother, and go to school.

Maud's high school in Prince Albert was very different from the one in Cavendish. It had once been a hotel. There were only nine

Maud's father and new wife. When Maud was 15, she went to live with the couple in Prince Albert, Saskatchewan

students in her class. Maud had to wear a real buffalo coat in winter, when the temperatures sometimes fell to forty-five degrees below zero. But she made new friends at school, in particular a boy named Willie. He was to be the first in a series of special boyfriends. She also had her first poem published back in P.E.I., in *The Charlottetown Examiner*.

When the school year ended, Maud decided to return home to Cavendish. She was unhappy at the thought of leaving her father, and was sad to part with her new friends. But she was glad to return to Prince Edward Island.

When she finished school in Cavendish, Maud went to Prince of Wales College in Charlottetown for her teacher's licence. Then she taught school for a year and saved $100 out of her salary of $180. It paid for her tuition and board at Dalhousie Ladies' College in Halifax,

Prince of Wales College

where she studied English Literature in the winter of 1895. In 1896, she won five dollars for the best letter on the question of who has more patience — a man or a woman. Her letter was in verse, and ended with the lines:

And while I admit it's true
That man has some patience, too,
And that woman isn't always sweetly calm,
Still, I think all must agree
On this central fact — that she
For general, all-round patience bears the palm.

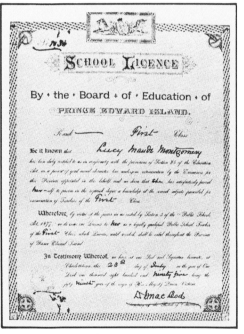

Maud, aged 19. She attended Prince of Wales College and earned two teaching certificates, a Second Class and a First Class

Publishing and Teaching

Lucy Maud continued to publish poems in Canada and the United States. She was one of the first well-paid female freelance writers in Canada. She was following the advice of one of her professors at teachers' college, who had told her that she had "great literary talent and should cultivate it."

For a few more years, she continued to teach. Sometimes she had as many as 60 children in her class. She rose early in the morning and wrote before her teaching day began. She also started to see her writing getting better. She wrote: "I know, by looking back, that I could not have written it six months, or a year, or four years ago, any more than I could have made a garment the material of which was still unwoven." Her professional writing career was taking flight just as her personal life started to collapse.

As Montgomery grew older she had many suitors. She was proposed to at least four times, and engaged once. But she fell in love only once, with a man called Herman Leard. She stopped his advances because she didn't think that they were suited to one another.

Sadly for Montgomery, before she could change her mind, fate played its hand. Her grandfather died. Montgomery returned to Cavendish to take care of her grandmother. Her

When her grandfather Macneill died in 1898, Maud gave up teaching and returned to live at Cavendish. She worked as assistant to the postmistress

friend, Willie, in Prince Albert died. Then, news reached Montgomery that Herman Leard had died from a serious illness. The final blow came when her father died in 1900. Montgomery wrote that she felt her life would never be the same again.

A Most Lovable Child

Montgomery then worked as a proofreader and writer at the Halifax *Daily Echo,* from the fall of 1901 to the summer of 1902. She learned to write in her spare time, amidst the noise of the printing presses and people coming and going. Somehow she managed to keep her own troubles out of her writing.

Montgomery always had difficulty starting a story. For her, writing the first paragraph equalled half the work of a whole story. Once the beginning was done, the rest came easily.

One day in 1902, Montgomery looked through her notebook, searching for an idea to start a series of stories for the newspaper. She found the now famous faded entry, "Elderly couple apply to orphan asylum for a boy. By mistake a girl is sent them." At the same time she remembered the picture of a young red-haired girl she had seen in a magazine. The character of Anne had started to take shape.

From the spring of 1904 to October 1905, Montgomery wrote *Anne of Green Gables*. Many of her own childhood memories went into it, including the beauty of Prince Edward Island and particular haunts such as Lover's Lane.

Montgomery typed the manuscript on an old typewriter that wouldn't type an M. She had to write the letter in the manuscript by hand.

The first page of *Anne of Green Gables*, as Maud first wrote it

When it was finished, she sent the manuscript to five publishing companies. They all sent it back. Discouraged, Montgomery packed it away in an old hat-box and forgot about it. Then one day when she was rummaging through some things, she came across the manuscript. She read it one more time. It didn't seem that bad. She mailed it to a sixth publisher.

This time the book was accepted. On June 28, 1908, *Anne of Green Gables* was published. Montgomery was 33 years old. She wrote, "Today has been, as Anne herself would say, 'an epoch in my life'."

Anne of Green Gables was an immediate best-seller. Maud was surprised and pleased

Anne of Green Gables

L. M. MONTGOMERY

The good stars met in your horoscope,
Made you of spirit and fire and dew.
—BROWNING

Toronto
THE RYERSON PRESS

A Great Writer

The public fell in love with Anne. Mark Twain wrote to say that Anne was "the dearest, and most lovable child in fiction since the immortal Alice". Montgomery wrote seven sequels to *Anne of Green Gables*, including *Anne of Avonlea* and *Anne of Ingleside*.

In some ways, Anne and Montgomery were very similar: imaginative, nature-loving, and emotional. Anne's habit of naming places was an old habit of Montgomery's. But Maud soon became tired of writing about Anne.

She decided to write a series of books on another character named Emily, whose soul was even closer to Montgomery's. Emily is a writer, unsure of her talent. She lives in a community that questions the suitability of a woman having a career as a writer. Emily gets engaged to one man, only to break off the engagement and marry the man she loves. Unfortunately, Montgomery's own life did not have such a romantic, happy ending.

Montgomery's favourite of all her books was *The Story Girl*. It was about a group of children from P.E.I. who loved to hear tales about their birthplace. Montgomery used her own family legends and experiences to create the book.

Anne of Avonlea was the first sequel to *Anne of Green Gables*. The 'Anne' books have been translated into many languages and are enjoyed all over the world

In 1911, Grandmother Macneill died. At thirty-seven, Montgomery was at last free to marry. But she chose a husband out of a sense of responsibility rather than love. She married Ewan Macdonald, a country minister, the same year. On her honeymoon, she fulfilled one of her life's dreams by visiting England and Scotland.

Maud waited until her grandmother died before she married Ewan Macdonald

The newly married Mr. & Mrs. Macdonald on their honeymoon in Scotland

When the couple returned, they moved to Leaskdale, Ontario, a little town 100 kilometres northeast of Toronto, where they lived for the next 15 years. They had two sons, Chester and Stuart. Montgomery spent most of her later life nursing her husband, taking care of the children, and doing church work. It was not an exciting life for her, but she had time to continue her writing.

In 1926, the family moved to Norval, just west of Toronto. By this time, she had published 15 books. In Norval, she helped local young people in producing plays, which were received with great delight. And there was always fan mail to answer. She wrote all her replies by

The Manse at Norval

hand, to Australia, China, and of course, to red-haired girls all over the world.

Ten years later, Ewan and Maud moved to Toronto, where they lived in a house that backed onto the Humber River. Both their sons went to university. But Maud suffered a bad attack of influenza, and then suffered a series of nervous breakdowns, from worry and from depression.

The Macdonald family, from left to right; Stuart, Reverend Macdonald, Lucy Maud Macdonald, Chester

"I love best the flowers I coax into bloom myself," said Maud

On April 24, 1942, Lucy Maud Montgomery died in Toronto. She was 68 and had published 21 novels and a book of poetry. She was the first Canadian author to be made a member of the Royal Society of Arts and Letters of London, England. King George V conferred on her the Order of the British Empire.

The young 14-year-old Prince Edward Island girl had kept her promise and her journal for over 50 years. Her journals, which have been published since her death, allow a rare insight into the development of a writer.

Many young people in other countries continue to get their first picture of Canada by reading *Anne Of Green Gables*. Every year, thousands of tourists visit the Old Macneill home — the original house of Green Gables in Prince Edward Island. And Lucy Maud Montgomery became what she had always dreamed of being: a great writer.

Anne of Green Gables is a well-loved and well-known character. She is portrayed in plays, movies, and even a postage stamp. Thousands tour Lucy Maud's childhood home every year

CHAPTER 5
Special People

Kids' writers are special people. They remember things most adults forget about growing up. They remember what was good and what was bad. They remember what made them afraid and what made them happy. They remember the things they used to think about and what was important to them. And they turn all those memories into wonderful stories.

Kids' writers write for all sorts of reasons. They write to make you laugh or to show you something in a new way. They also write because they love telling stories. They remember how important books were when they were children.

In some ways, Dennis Lee, Robert Munsch, Lucy Maud Montgomery, and Jean Little are not very much alike. They have different personalities, different lives, and different ways of telling a story. But in over 60 books altogether, they are alike in having created something very special for children. They have opened new doors for other Canadian kids' writers, and they have won loyal fans around the world. Best of all, they have never forgotten what it's like to be a child.

THE POETRY OF LUCY MAUD MONTGOMERY

CONTEMPORARY CANADIAN BIOGRAPHIES

Her Special Vision

A BIOGRAPHY OF JEAN LITTLE

BY BARBARA GREENWOOD AND AUDREY MCKIM

There are two sides to this poet
--the fuzzy, rumpled side that kids
and the other side: sharper, dar

DENNIS LEE:
MAN AND BOY